Wonderful Wacky Words

God Wants You to Remember

ISBN: 978-1-59842-904-6

Wonderful Wacky Women.

Inspiring•Uplifting•Empowering

is a trademark of Suzy and Al Toronto. Used under license.

M and Blue Mountain Press are registered in U.S. Patent and Trademark Office. Certain trademarks are used under license.

Printed in China.
Fifth Printing: 2018

⊕ This book is printed on recycled paper.

This book is printed on paper that has been specially produced to be acid free (neutral pH) and contains no groundwood or unbleached pulp. It conforms with the requirements of the American National Standards Institute, Inc., so as to ensure that this book will last and be enjoyed by future generations.

Blue Mountain Arts, Inc.
P.O. Box 4549, Boulder, Colorado 80306

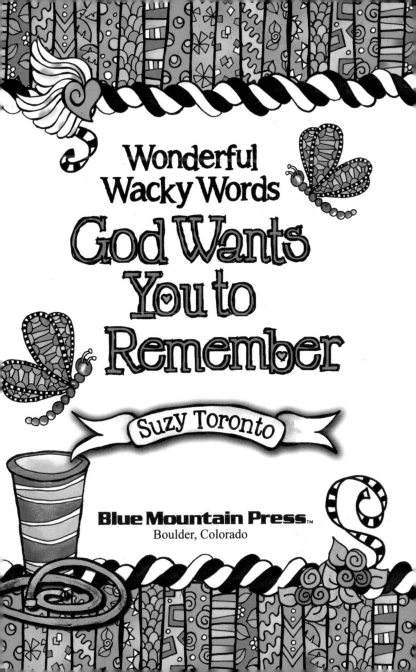

Wonderful
Wacky Words
God Wants
You to
Remember

Suzy Toronto

Blue Mountain Press™
Boulder, Colorado

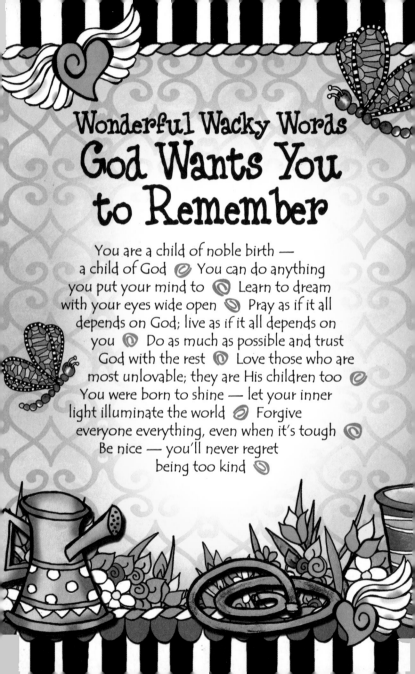

Wonderful Wacky Words
God Wants You to Remember

You are a child of noble birth —
a child of God ✺ You can do anything
you put your mind to ✺ Learn to dream
with your eyes wide open ✺ Pray as if it all
depends on God; live as if it all depends on
you ✺ Do as much as possible and trust
God with the rest ✺ Love those who are
most unlovable; they are His children too ✺
You were born to shine — let your inner
light illuminate the world ✺ Forgive
everyone everything, even when it's tough ✺
Be nice — you'll never regret
being too kind ✺

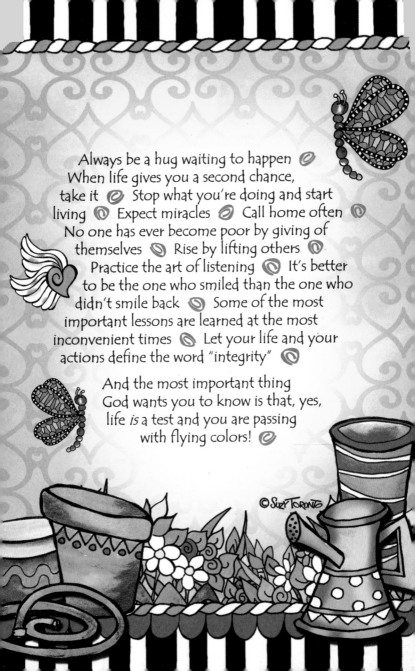

Always be a hug waiting to happen
When life gives you a second chance,
take it   Stop what you're doing and start
living   Expect miracles   Call home often
No one has ever become poor by giving of
themselves   Rise by lifting others
Practice the art of listening   It's better
to be the one who smiled than the one who
didn't smile back   Some of the most
important lessons are learned at the most
inconvenient times   Let your life and your
actions define the word "integrity"

And the most important thing
God wants you to know is that, yes,
life *is* a test and you are passing
with flying colors!

© Suzy Toronto

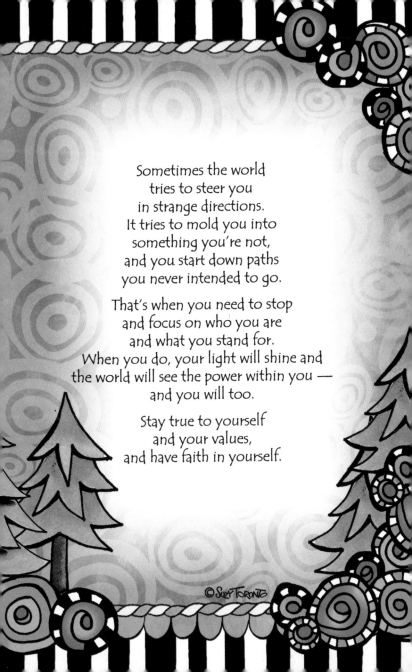

Sometimes the world
tries to steer you
in strange directions.
It tries to mold you into
something you're not,
and you start down paths
you never intended to go.

That's when you need to stop
and focus on who you are
and what you stand for.
When you do, your light will shine and
the world will see the power within you —
and you will too.

Stay true to yourself
and your values,
and have faith in yourself.

© Suzy Toronto

Somehow you manage to stay
genuine and unaffected
by the whims of the world,
even when surrounded by "imitations."
You seem to always have perfect clarity
about who you are and what you stand for.
And the more you shine,
the more others want
to live up to your standards.

What a gift you have,
and what a gift you share!

How to Live a Life Worth Loving

Just Stop, Listen, and Learn

Stop. Stop churning through those endless, pointless cycles that blind you from appreciating that the world around you is so much bigger than your immediate crisis. Stop focusing inward, and look beyond yourself. Stop ignoring the rich opportunities for growth that you've passed up, simply because you were afraid. Stop hauling around your unnecessary baggage — whether it's emotional or physical. Unburden yourself from the constant repetition of reliving each mistake or wrong done to you. None of it serves to inspire, uplift, or empower another human being... least of all you!

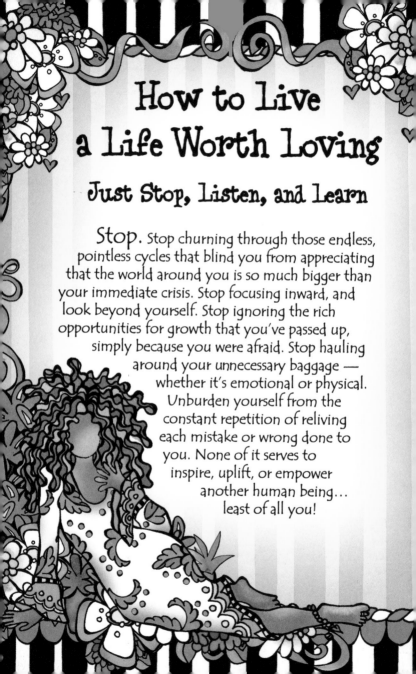

Listen. Listen to your breathing, to your heartbeat. Listen to the sound of the ocean, the rustle of leaves in the wind, and the silence of softly falling snow.
Stop talking… and really take the time to just listen. Seek out those who have accomplished astonishing feats, and listen to what they have to say. Absorb all that is good in them, and let the rest drift away. Drink in the wisdom they have to offer. Such wisdom is everywhere, if you will just open your heart and listen…

©Suzy Toronto

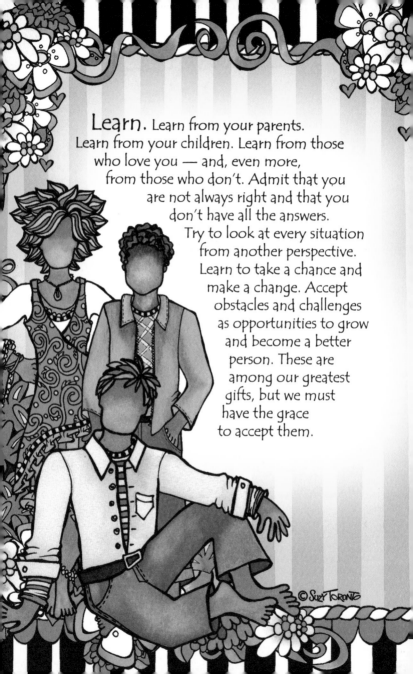

Learn. Learn from your parents. Learn from your children. Learn from those who love you — and, even more, from those who don't. Admit that you are not always right and that you don't have all the answers. Try to look at every situation from another perspective. Learn to take a chance and make a change. Accept obstacles and challenges as opportunities to grow and become a better person. These are among our greatest gifts, but we must have the grace to accept them.

© Suzy Toronto

Here's the real irony of life:
in order for growth to be all about you,
you have to stop thinking about yourself,
listen to the wisdom of those around you,
and learn from it all.

See?
It's easy.

Just stop, listen,
and learn.

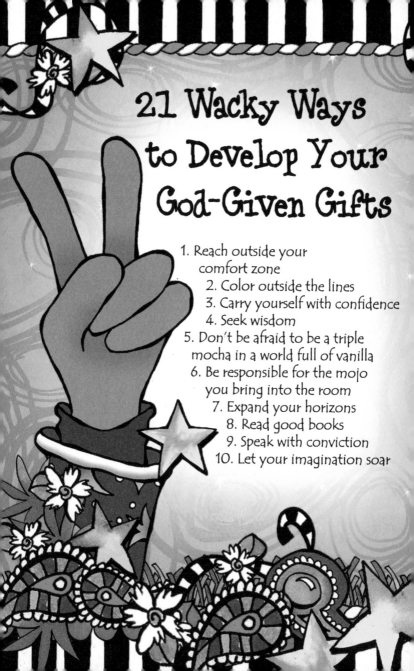

21 Wacky Ways to Develop Your God-Given Gifts

1. Reach outside your comfort zone
2. Color outside the lines
3. Carry yourself with confidence
4. Seek wisdom
5. Don't be afraid to be a triple mocha in a world full of vanilla
6. Be responsible for the mojo you bring into the room
7. Expand your horizons
8. Read good books
9. Speak with conviction
10. Let your imagination soar

11. Believe that your future does not lie ahead of you; it lies deep inside you
12. Don't let someone who gave up on their dreams talk you out of yours
13. Choose the right thing… even when it's not the easiest choice
14. Develop an attitude of gratitude
15. Live with integrity
16. Make your life and your actions a story worth telling
17. Stay focused… you only see obstacles when you take your eyes off the goal
18. Choose to make virtue a habit
19. Dream in colors that do not yet exist
20. Create the life you've always wanted
21. Always believe that something fabulously amazing is going to happen

© Suzy Toronto

If You Only Pray When You're in Trouble... You're in Trouble!

Prayer is a mighty thing. You know it
as well as I do. But often it's not until
our world starts to crumble
and we're about to go down
in flames that it finally
dawns on us to ask for help
from a power that is
greater than ourselves.
When we just can't stand
anymore, we finally realize
we need to kneel.

© Suzy Toronto

When did God become our last resort
instead of our first defense?
When did we decide we'd only pray
once we'd run out of options
instead of making it a foundation of our daily lives?
What if we made prayer a priority right now,
as if He is #1 on our celestial speed dial?
The truth is there are always five bars glowing
on our heavenly cell phones.

Living a life filled with prayer can
strengthen us beyond our abilities and give us
an understanding beyond our comprehension.
It infuses us with courage and hope
and allows us to create a life worth loving
despite the challenges we may face.

So give it a try... and do not delay.
Bottom line, if you only pray
when you're in trouble,
bless your heart...
you're in trouble.

The Challenges
We Face
Can Be
So Tough...

I often wonder
why some people
seem to have more
than their fair share
of challenges.
I guess I'm going to
have to keep wondering
because, bottom line,
there is no answer.

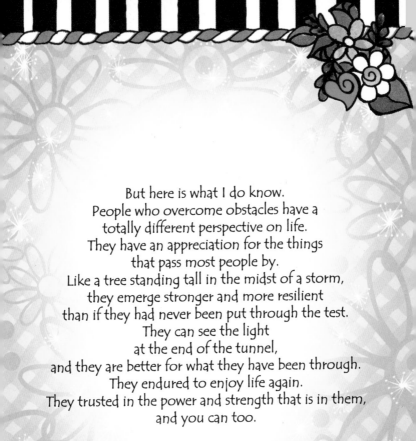

But here is what I do know.
People who overcome obstacles have a
totally different perspective on life.
They have an appreciation for the things
that pass most people by.
Like a tree standing tall in the midst of a storm,
they emerge stronger and more resilient
than if they had never been put through the test.
They can see the light
at the end of the tunnel,
and they are better for what they have been through.
They endured to enjoy life again.
They trusted in the power and strength that is in them,
and you can too.

© Suzy Toronto

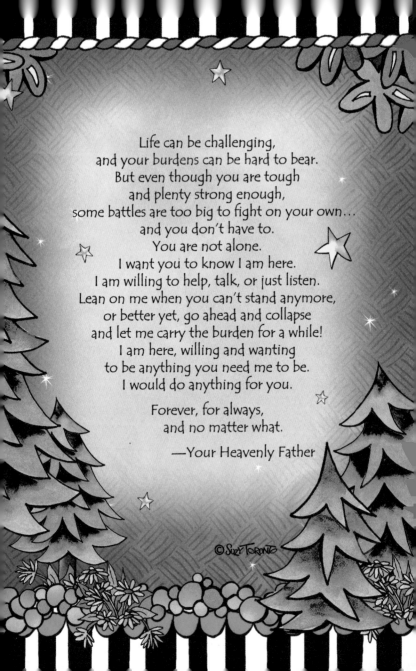

Life can be challenging,
and your burdens can be hard to bear.
But even though you are tough
and plenty strong enough,
some battles are too big to fight on your own…
and you don't have to.
You are not alone.
I want you to know I am here.
I am willing to help, talk, or just listen.
Lean on me when you can't stand anymore,
or better yet, go ahead and collapse
and let me carry the burden for a while!
I am here, willing and wanting
to be anything you need me to be.
I would do anything for you.

Forever, for always,
and no matter what.

—Your Heavenly Father

©Suzy Toronto

Live Your Life with

NO REGRETS

No one wants to be constantly saying
"would've, should've, could've"...
forever looking back,
second-guessing every decision,
and fretting over
what might have been.
Yet it's funny how we
can cling to the past,
thinking that if we dwell
on it long enough
we can actually find
a "do over" button
and create a whole
different ending.

Daily ★ News

THE PAST IS OVER

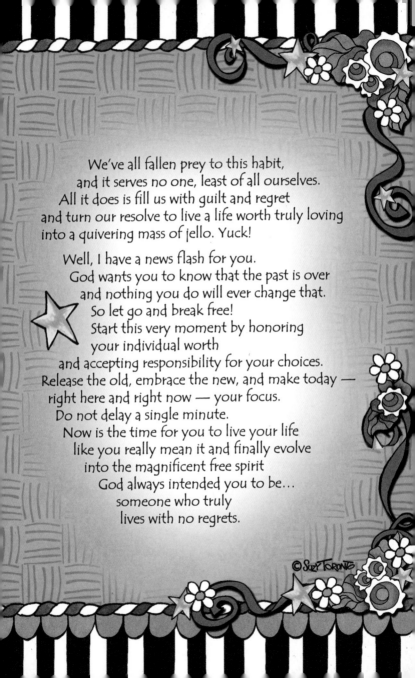

We've all fallen prey to this habit,
and it serves no one, least of all ourselves.
All it does is fill us with guilt and regret
and turn our resolve to live a life worth truly loving
into a quivering mass of jello. Yuck!

Well, I have a news flash for you.
God wants you to know that the past is over
and nothing you do will ever change that.
So let go and break free!
Start this very moment by honoring
your individual worth
and accepting responsibility for your choices.
Release the old, embrace the new, and make today —
right here and right now — your focus.
Do not delay a single minute.
Now is the time for you to live your life
like you really mean it and finally evolve
into the magnificent free spirit
God always intended you to be...
someone who truly
lives with no regrets.

© Suzy Toronto

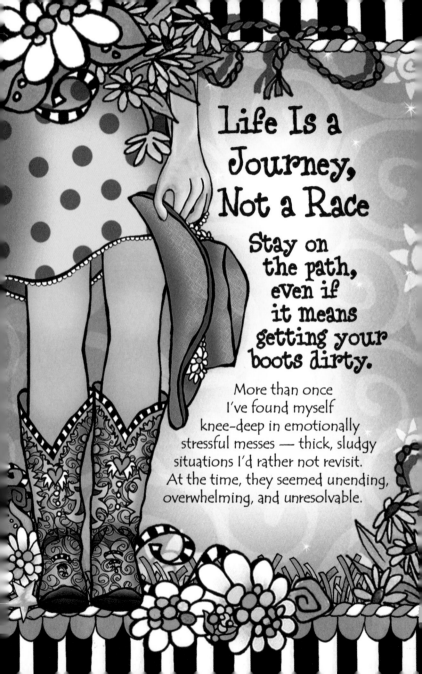

Life Is a Journey, Not a Race

Stay on the path, even if it means getting your boots dirty.

More than once
I've found myself
knee-deep in emotionally
stressful messes — thick, sludgy
situations I'd rather not revisit.
At the time, they seemed unending,
overwhelming, and unresolvable.

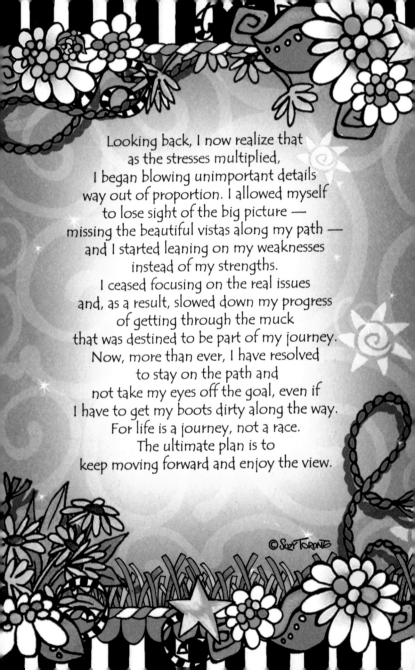

Looking back, I now realize that
as the stresses multiplied,
I began blowing unimportant details
way out of proportion. I allowed myself
to lose sight of the big picture —
missing the beautiful vistas along my path —
and I started leaning on my weaknesses
instead of my strengths.
I ceased focusing on the real issues
and, as a result, slowed down my progress
of getting through the muck
that was destined to be part of my journey.
Now, more than ever, I have resolved
to stay on the path and
not take my eyes off the goal, even if
I have to get my boots dirty along the way.
For life is a journey, not a race.
The ultimate plan is to
keep moving forward and enjoy the view.

© Suzy Toronto

In a World Where Bigger Is Always Better...
Think Small!

Sometimes we all think big way too much.
Don't get me wrong — thinking up really big,
wild, and crazy ideas is one of my favorite things to do.
But life is also about finding the simple things that
take our breath away and illuminate our tiny corner
of the world. These tender moments give our
lives deeper meaning and sometimes become
our most treasured memories. Quite simply...
they make our hearts tingle.

It's moments like nuzzling a newborn baby's cheek and vowing never to forget that sweet smell. Or sitting on a porch swing with your grandmother and praying you'll always remember her voice. It's laughing at a silly joke between friends and hearing the echo of your own childhood giggles. It's watching a parade with a lump in your throat and your hand on your heart when the vets go by. It's waking up in the morning and really feeling grateful for one more day.

It's easy to get caught up in the rapture of life's brilliant, amazing, and spectacular things. But in the end, we must always remember that life is really no big thing... it's a zillion little things, just waiting to be cherished. Now take a deep breath... and feel the tingle!

© Suzy Toronto

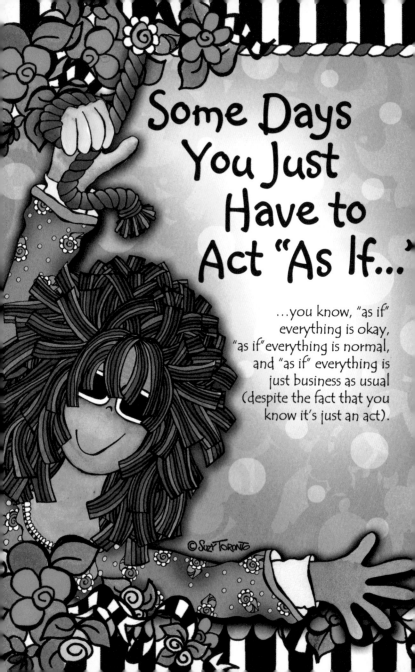

Some Days
You Just
Have to
Act "As If..."

...you know, "as if"
everything is okay,
"as if" everything is normal,
and "as if" everything is
just business as usual
(despite the fact that you
know it's just an act).

© Suzy Toronto

Some people call it "fake it till you make it,"
but I like to think of it more as acting with faith.
It's about believing in something you can't see or touch.
It's about reaching deeper into yourself than ever before
to find your true strength and courage…
even if they're right alongside doubt and fear.
And it's about ignoring the voices around you
that tell you to give up.

Think of it this way:
What if just around the next corner
a shiny brass ring is waiting for you?
What if the rainbow's end is just around the bend,
its pot of gold emblazoned with your name?
What if you act "as if" for just one more minute?
This is not the time to wimp out and be a chicken.
This is the time to press forward with faith.
This is the time to put on your game face
and act "as if" nothing were impossible.
When you do, you will stand tall
with conviction and pride, knowing you have
finally created the life you've always imagined.

Wonderful Wacky Words...
Faith, Hope, and Wisdom

Remember, if you want rainbows, you gotta have rain ✿ When nothing else works, never underestimate the power of chocolate ✿ It's okay to cry ✿ Embrace change ✿ Take the day off to master the art of doing nothing ✿ Life is all about how you handle Plan B — in the end it will be the truest test of your character ✿ To expect a miracle, you first must believe in them ✿ Smile even when it hurts ✿

© Suzy Toronto

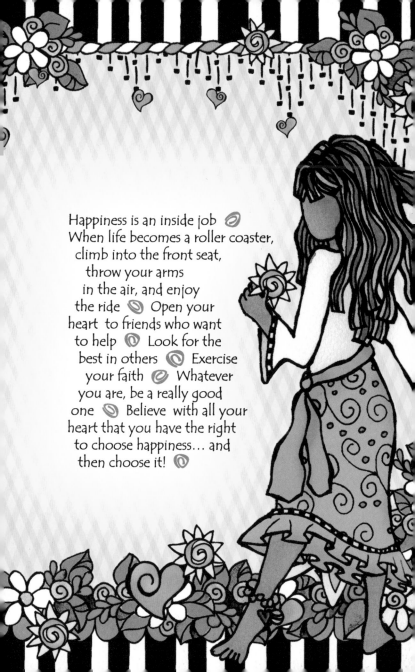

Happiness is an inside job When life becomes a roller coaster, climb into the front seat, throw your arms in the air, and enjoy the ride Open your heart to friends who want to help Look for the best in others Exercise your faith Whatever you are, be a really good one Believe with all your heart that you have the right to choose happiness… and then choose it!

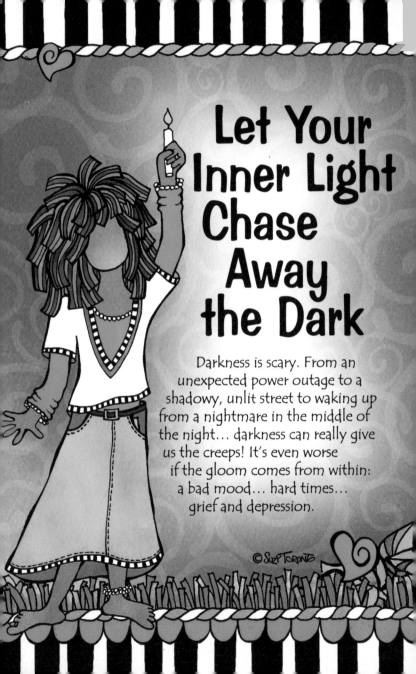

Let Your Inner Light Chase Away the Dark

Darkness is scary. From an unexpected power outage to a shadowy, unlit street to waking up from a nightmare in the middle of the night… darkness can really give us the creeps! It's even worse if the gloom comes from within: a bad mood… hard times… grief and depression.

©Suzy Toronto

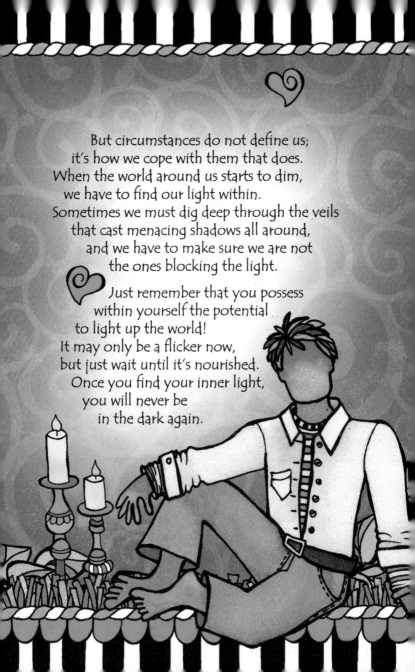

But circumstances do not define us;
it's how we cope with them that does.
When the world around us starts to dim,
we have to find our light within.
Sometimes we must dig deep through the veils
that cast menacing shadows all around,
and we have to make sure we are not
the ones blocking the light.

Just remember that you possess
within yourself the potential
to light up the world!
It may only be a flicker now,
but just wait until it's nourished.
Once you find your inner light,
you will never be
in the dark again.

Sometimes life gives you a second chance.
Right in the middle of what seems like
a big bunch of muck,
a shiny brass ring appears
within your reach,
giving you a chance to start over.

Do not back away or question
whether it's your turn;
reach out with all the belief you've got.
Grab ahold of that ring for all it's worth
and never let go!

Miracles do happen,
and sometimes life does give you
a second chance.
So don't wait one second longer…
take it!

© Suzy Toronto

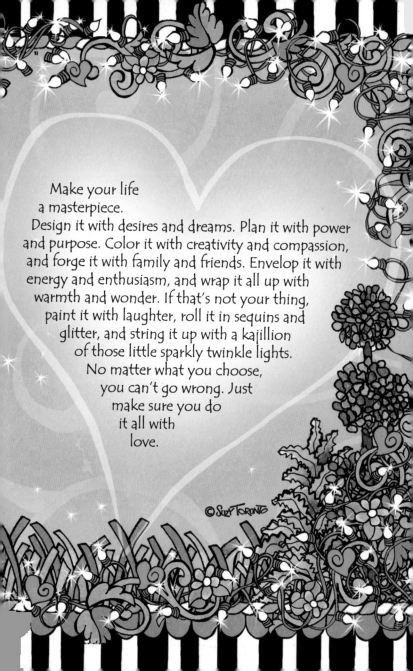

Make your life
a masterpiece.
Design it with desires and dreams. Plan it with power
and purpose. Color it with creativity and compassion,
and forge it with family and friends. Envelop it with
energy and enthusiasm, and wrap it all up with
warmth and wonder. If that's not your thing,
paint it with laughter, roll it in sequins and
glitter, and string it up with a kajillion
of those little sparkly twinkle lights.
No matter what you choose,
you can't go wrong. Just
make sure you do
it all with
love.

© Suzy Toronto

You Are Surrounded by Angels

Legions of angels surround you every day helping you on your journey Angels comfort you when you're down and encourage you when you struggle The best angels give you what you need, not what you want — even if that's a good, swift kick!

© Suzy Toronto

Angels are better at cheering than jeering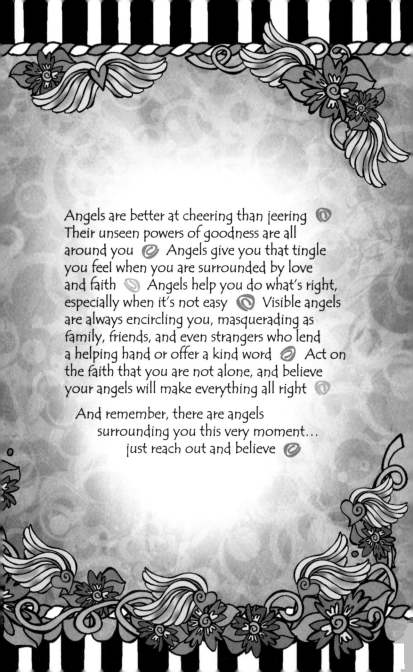
Their unseen powers of goodness are all
around you 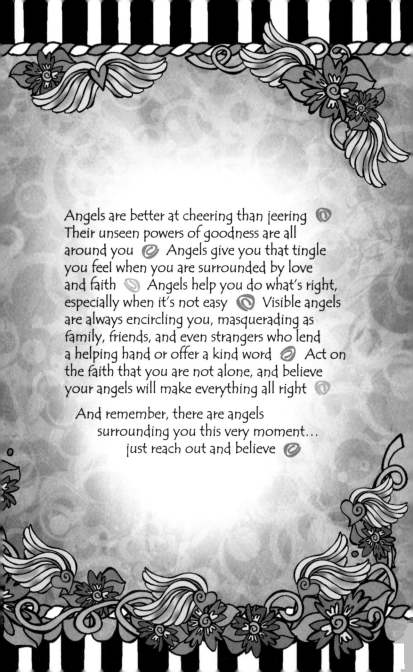 Angels give you that tingle
you feel when you are surrounded by love
and faith Angels help you do what's right,
especially when it's not easy Visible angels
are always encircling you, masquerading as
family, friends, and even strangers who lend
a helping hand or offer a kind word Act on
the faith that you are not alone, and believe
your angels will make everything all right

And remember, there are angels
surrounding you this very moment...
just reach out and believe

About the Author

So this is me… I'm a tad wacky and just shy of crazy. I'm fiftysomething and live in the sleepy village of Tangerine, Florida, with my husband, Al, and a big, goofy dog named Lucy. And because life wasn't crazy enough, my eightysomething-year-old parents live with us too. (In my home, the nuts don't fall far from the tree!) I eat far too much chocolate, and I drink sparkling water by the gallon. I practice yoga, ride a little red scooter, and go to the beach every chance I get. I have five grown children and over a dozen grandkids who love me as much as I adore them. I teach them to dip their French fries in their chocolate shakes and to make up any old words to the tunes they like. But most of all, I teach them to never, ever color inside the lines. This is the Wild Wacky Wonderful life I lead, and I wouldn't have it any other way. Welcome to my world!